Homespun Tapestry

Also by Brenda Eldridge and published by Ginninderra Press

Poetry

The Silver Cord

It's All Good

A Personal View

Facing Cancer

From My Garden

Best Heard & Seen

Scarves

Tangled Roots: new & selected poems

Wonderment

Elemental (Pocket Poets)

Forgotten Dreams (Pocket Poets)

Big Blue Marble (Pocket Poets)

Not What They Might Seem (Picaro Poets)

Non-fiction

Down by the River

Tales From My Patagonia

It's Still Out There

There's a Rainbow Serpent In My Garden

Eastwards

From Patagonia to Australia

Forty Green (Pocket Places)

Who Was She? (Pocket People)

Dear Dad (Pocket People)

Edited by Brenda Eldridge and published by Ginninderra Press

Brave Enough To Be a Poet

The Heart of Port Adelaide

Collecting Writers

Brenda Eldridge

Homespun Tapestry

Homespun Tapestry
ISBN 978 1 76041 231 9
Copyright © text Brenda Eldridge 2016
Cover photo: Brenda Eldridge

First published 2016 by
Ginninderra Press
PO Box 3461 Port Adelaide 5015
www.ginninderrapress.com.au

Contents

Introduction	7
Home	9
Children	15
Fear	19
Friendship	23
Desert emptiness	27
Solitude and silence	31
Spirituality	35
Tolerance	43
Immediate joy	49
Wholeness	55

Introduction

There have been many times in my life when I have felt the need to take stock. I've pondered over what is in my life and how the past meshes with the present, and the awareness this brings, in turn, colours the future.

Writing in my journal every day keeps some clarity in my thoughts but it isn't always enough. I had a goal in mind when I began writing this series of essays. I have long loved Kahlil Gibran's *The Prophet* and I fancied doing my own version. In *The Prophet*, the narrator lived on the edges of a community for years and at the point of leaving he was asked for his observations of the lives of those in the community.

Unlike Gibran, I am not suggesting a philosophy for anyone else to live their life by. I am writing from my own experiences. I found my topics ran into each other and there were no clearly defined borders. This means in the reading there are thoughts or situations that appear several times and not in chronological order.

There is no particular order to the essays. Each one stands alone. I wrote as the mood took me and the computer sorted them alphabetically – without being asked. I decided to jumble them up, only choosing the placement of the first and last.

Choosing a title was through my usual process of elimination. Many years ago when I was working, someone said, if you want 'tea and sympathy' go and see Brenda. Then I coined my own phrase of 'kitchen sink philosophy'. My life is a wonderfully rich tapestry of dark and light so what better to call this collection than *Homespun Tapestry*.

Home

What makes a home?

Like most things in my life, I learned by a process of elimination the kind of home I wanted for myself and my children. I hadn't realised just how peaceful my home had been as a child, and for me the best part of that was going home at the end of a school day or work and being able to just 'be'. No one required me to perform. There were the usual expectations: an unspoken code of good manners, keeping feet off the chairs, taking used dishes back to the kitchen and so on. Perhaps it was because my parents were quiet people anyway, but quiet evenings are among my special memories. When television came into our home, I was about twelve; this timed well with teenagers and our desire for music – the 60s were extraordinary for innovative sounds.

When my children's father, our two sons and I arrived in Australia, living in migrant hostels for six months, I listened to other women looking forward to having a home and talking about what furniture they would buy. We had no money and were dependent on the Salvation Army or its equivalent for even the basics, such as beds and tables and chairs. To his credit, my children's father remedied this as quickly as he was able but I had learned that I cared little for the trappings that supposedly made a home. Subconsciously perhaps, I knew that it was something else I hungered for.

I wanted home to be the place where we could all retreat from the demands of the outside world. Yes, I was trying to emulate my childhood home where all our furniture was second-hand and it didn't seem to matter. I also found with three small boys that the simpler the contents of a home, the less could get broken and the easier it was to keep clean and tidy. I was far more interested in the luxury of a washing machine than a fancy couch. Oh, such bliss with so much washing, even if at first it was only a round one with a ringer, to be later upgraded to a twin-tub. Even after forty-five years, I love that I can put washing out almost any time of year and it will be dry the same day!

Creating a home is very much linked to who we are, or how we see ourselves. It wasn't till 1989, when I left my marriage and moved out of the family home to set up a home for myself, that I became fully aware of this.

Once again I had very little money and only basic items were bought. I rather liked sleeping on a mattress on the floor. It was new and the sheets and quilt covers were all new and the floral patterns that I wanted. I wasn't buying anything to please a partner or to be fashionable. I lived in a small flat and I liked that, though I was too distressed by circumstances to really enjoy it. I always had at least one of my sons living with me at any time. It was enough to be away from constant conflict and noisy television or intrusive voices. However, David S came into my life at this time.

A few months after my son Mark died in 1991, I moved on and found the tree house. It was a strange little two-bedroom house but I loved every inch of it. The tree house was in the foot hills north-east of Adelaide. It was nestled on a hillside and the trees at the bottom of the garden were very tall and stately and I seemed to be living in the treetops themselves. I could look out of my window directly into the eyes of a koala or owl. The river ran only a few metres below and I grew to love all its moods with the changing seasons. I shared the tree house with David S at first. He had bullied his way into my life but in fairness there was an important place for him. He taught me literally how to survive and while I don't ever want or need to talk about him or our time together it was significant in the scheme of things.

My children's father had wanted to dominate our lives and destroyed all harmony in the home with his need to lecture us and exercise his power over us: his way or no way. He would not allow me to embrace him in the home and haven I tried to create for myself and my sons. He drove me from my home and family.

David S wasn't like that, but he did absolutely nothing to create anything in our life together. He was given no choice but to leave the Public Service (where we had met) because of his health (insulin-dependent diabetes, epilepsy controlled by medication, and very damaged eyesight; the last two were from a childhood accident). He was placed on a blind disability pension which gave him an income, but I was expected to support us by paying the rent and utilities and groceries. He did nothing in the way of housework even after he stopped work, and could see nothing strange about what I called unequal distribution of chores. When challenged, he said his father had refused to help with dishes or make the bed even though his wife worked full-time, so he wasn't going to either. I had neither energy or inclination to argue but it did make it easier when I finally said enough and ended the relationship and he was the one to leave to go back to living with his mother. His only comment when I ended it was to say he thought he was fixed up for life. This brings some very unpleasant thoughts about him and I will not go further down that path. Enough to say he left and I started living alone – which lasted for ten years.

At last I could make a home just for myself. I still wasn't interested in material things. My minimal furniture was all I needed to be comfortable. My TV had a small screen and I rarely watched it; rather it was needed to watch DVDs I borrowed from the local library. I took up painting again and I became surrounded by an explosion of colour. I grew indoor plants – something I had not ever done before. I could put things down and they stayed put till I chose to move them again – no helpful little hands interfering with paints or writing materials left on the table. I cooked just to suit myself, which turned out to be very unadventurous. Eating was something I had to do to have the energy to do other things.

But it wasn't all pleasure. If I went away for a trip, say to visit Annette in Canberra, in her home I was looked after, cosseted; someone else did the cooking and provided transport and ideas where to go. I felt safe. Then came the time to go home. There was no one waiting for me at the airport. There was no one waiting for me at the door with the kettle on for a welcome-home cuppa. There was no one to welcome me home. But this was true of every day, whether I went to work, to the shops, or out for the day. I came home to an empty house. I used to walk in and say, 'Hello, house.' Something no doubt many people who have or do live alone will admit to was the naming of items in the house. My cycle was called Beatrice and my car Pegasus. I talked to myself a lot when making something to eat or deciding what movie to watch. I listened to countless talking books.

When I was going out for the day or away for a brief holiday, I used to let my eldest son, Alex, know and when I would be back so it would be noted if I was missing.

When I had a hysterectomy, I was in hospital for six days and only allowed home then because Annette came over from Canberra to stay with me for a week so I would not be alone. But after she left I was alone for another five weeks, not able to go to work. I was deeply shocked that my family didn't contact me much to see if I was all right.

It was from then that I started feeling vulnerable living alone but I still knew I preferred that to living with the wrong person. I had done that for almost thirty years of my life one way and another and I promised myself I would not ever do it again.

My son Noel J lived out away from the suburbs and had a self-contained granny flat at the back of his house. I used to tease him that it was my retirement villa. He did not like me living alone, and said I should at least have a dog. I am terrified of dogs and countered with 'Couldn't I have a turtle?' He wasn't really amused.

Again, fairness demands that I say the tree house was not child-friendly. The garden was not enclosed fully by fences. I didn't mind, but it meant little ones could escape. Because the land was on a steep slope, there was an assortment of steps to navigate everywhere and little ones could so easily fall and hurt themselves, so visiting Grandma was fraught with difficulties. It was theoretically much easier for me to visit them, but I found that very hard. The two older boys had partners who had very different ideas about housework from mine. I would never win a house-proud award but I hated to see the unwashed dishes and general litter everywhere; there seemed to be little effort made to provide what I would call a home. I can come at untidiness, especially when there are children, but not dirtiness and an air of not caring.

So what did I want in my home?

Always a haven from the outside world, without doubt. I worked for the Public Service for twenty-five years. I met people from all walks of life who showed amazing richness or poverty of spirit. I had time for all of them within that restricted environment, but I didn't want any of that in my home.

Silence. There is far too much aimless chatter wherever we go these days. A trip to the shops entails being bombarded with music and voices. Radio and television can provide entertainment but an awful lot of rubbish too. I have always felt the best thing about a television is the off switch.

A garden. Oh, how I love to have a garden. Not too big like the one at the tree house. That was just too much for me alone. I have a wonderful garden now. But I am going too fast.

The last thing I want to mention about my tree house is my visitors. I could simply admit they were my lovers, but something in me these days is more circumspect. I am not ashamed or embarrassed but it is laying myself open to judgement. I had beautiful visitors and for a couple of hours or so I could forget I was alone and hungered for anything different. I gave my lovers what they no longer were getting at home from their wives. I did it deliberately. I decided that if they were going to risk everything to be with me, then I was going to make it at least feel like it was worthwhile.

The heartache it brought me was that they loved to visit but no one wanted to stay. Whatever I made them feel, I suspect they took the benefits of that back to their home and families. Perhaps I even made them appreciate their families more. But I grew tired of being someone's secret smile while they read the newspaper or watched boring television. I didn't want to be someone they couldn't be seen with, and only shared time with me inside my tree house. It was as if they were ashamed of what they were doing. For a long time I thought they risked everything to be with me but would give nothing up to be with me. I suspect that I was kidding no one but myself. None of them ever said we would have a life together. Even my brother envied me my independence and seemed to conveniently overlook the times of desperate loneliness.

So once again I said, 'No more.' Into this space stepped Stephen and a totally different life.

We rent a house, which proves home is nothing to do with owning bricks and mortar. My son David said something like that. He was like me and had not ever wanted to buy house. Then he met Amy and he knew she was his home. He needed to buy a house to put his home in.

I have someone to share my life with who wants to share their life with me equally as much. I don't know how it is that we can be so easy living together. We both love silence and reading. We both enjoy watching old movies and listening to similar music. Stephen loves to cook and I am more than happy to let him. He does the vacuuming. I do the washing and ironing. We didn't sit down and divide the chores, we seemed to fall into a pattern. We both love pottering in the garden. I grow the flowers, herbs and vegetables, Stephen trims the hedges and chooses the native plants. We are alike in many ways and both don't want conflict or disharmony in our lives. We talk about everything, so there are very rarely misunderstandings. Tolerance is a major part of the success of our relationship and our lives together.

Home. I know what I had as a child. I know what I had with my children and their father. I know what I had when I lived in the right house but with the wrong person. I know what I had when I lived alone and had nice visitors. I know what I hungered for. I know that I have found what I hungered for.

Children

As I typed the title for this essay, I immediately thought of *The Prophet* by Kahlil Gibran, and I am not in the same category as him. The most obvious reason is that he was male and even if he was a father he couldn't write from a mother's perspective. That doesn't make his thoughts any less valid, I just think he would have had a different experience of children and I can only write from my own.

I was so young when I became a mother. Not just in years but in maturity. I had done nothing to discover who I was as a person except that I knew I liked to paint and read historical novels. I didn't really have much self-awareness. Having said that, I can say I have been blessed with the opportunity of self-discovery because of my children. I find no appeal in trying to speculate what person I would have become without them.

I loved the world through my children's eyes. I was as thrilled as they were at the discovery of furry caterpillars and vegetables growing… I was lucky that wherever we lived there was always a natural world for them to play in. They weren't bound in suburbia; we were lucky enough to live on the outer edges of the two different estates – but it wasn't country life as I knew it.

I have been reading some essays written by my brother and the first one, giving his chapbook its title, is *From Humble Beginnings*. Like me, Geoff has fond memories of growing up in an old ramshackle house with no modern amenities but access to endless acres of woods, orchards and meadows. When he writes of these familiar places, I am with him.

And so it was with my own children. Yes, in a country on the far side of the planet from where I grew up, but I can see now that, by sharing their world of exploration and wonder, I was reliving my own happy childhood. I encouraged them to look for the unusual and to see the beauty in everything.

The sweetest gifts they gave me were a handful of wild flowers, an oddly coloured stone or shells… I recall a neighbour giving one of them a bouquet of roses from her garden for me for Mother's Day – so he wouldn't pinch them when she was not watching and probably damage the bush.

I find it indescribably sad that I cannot recall being filled with inner peace or serenity when I was pregnant with my babies. Either too young, or too afraid or because of my circumstances, I remember for the most part feeling very isolated. My unborn children did not provide me with company as such, but I did feel very protective of each of them. I felt once they were born that they were no longer mine. Perhaps other women in different circumstances share their hopes and fears with their child's father and so experience pregnancy in a very different way.

I suspect my experiences were all too familiar and I wonder if perhaps that is part of why becoming a grandmother is so rewarding for some. The chance to share the awaited arrival of the child of their child. All the pleasure and not too much of the responsibilities. Time for endless hugs and storytelling, going for walks and playing on the beach. Shopping not fraught with things you can't afford to buy, forever having to say no. I have not been this kind of grandmother. I was too afraid to hold them in my arms and get too attached because they weren't my children.

I wonder if having only sons has coloured my view. If I had been blessed with a daughter, would I have shared her hopes and fears during pregnancy? Does having the child of your child when your child is a daughter have a different sense of connection than the all-male regime I have known? Not even one granddaughter! There must be a reason for all these males in my life. My brothers have all had daughters – well, one each at least. My sons too have lamented that they have not had daughters.

I am in the privileged position of viewing childhood from several perspectives. My own childhood was happy, and troublesome issues only occurred when I was about nine or ten and it was time for me to be more socially active. I have the memories of when my own children were small. I have memories – limited, it cannot be denied – of my grandchildren growing up.

Now I can acknowledge the hunger in my arms to hold a tiny baby. To feel that soft sleepy-heaviness as they drift into sleep. I have wandered sometimes along the path of what-ifs: having a child when I was older and not having to share with another parent. Common sense and life have taught me that parenting really is best with a mother and father, but that didn't stop me dreaming a little. In an ideal world, whatever that is.

I like the things I have read about the North American natives. Children were in the care of all the people in the village or tribe. It has been that way for Australian Aborigines but I can't forget that much of the time they were hungry simply because of the harsh conditions of this land. But I love the notion of not being alone caring for a newborn who can only cry to let you know it needs something. Having older wiser women who would welcome the opportunity to help and teach.

I realise this way of extended families was all over the world in all cultures in the days when the elders of the family lived out their time in the heart of their family and revered for their knowledge and wisdom. I know too that it must not have been ideal all of the time, but perhaps with a slower pace of living there was more patience and more tolerance.

Fear

It has been years since I have felt the need to flee from a place. Stephen has held me safe. He has done so much in the few years we have been together to ease the fears and terrors I have lived with all my adult life. Why has it all crumbled this afternoon?

The event today is readings from the social justice anthology *First Refuge*.

I know social justice drives Stephen a lot; perhaps more than anything else, it has kept him running Ginninderra Press – his way of rebelling, or fighting for everything he believes in. Voices of ordinary people needing to be heard – he has given them this. And I am included in those numbers. As an editor of my own series, I am an active and publicly acknowledged member of what Stephen is all about. Yesterday he stood in front of a hundred people and declared that he not only couldn't but wouldn't want to continue without me.

Yet here I am today cowering in the coffee shop next to East Avenue Books where all this is going on.

A year ago at our friends' birthday celebration, I was in a conversation with Ann Nadge, the editor of *First Refuge*. I told her that I find the whole issue of social justice or lack of it too big to be able to deal with. She was quite insistent that I write about that. And I did. I sent it in and as far as I was concerned that was to be the end of it.

Since then I have come out and said on a few occasions in public that poets are the untarnished voice of our community and I am proud to call myself a poet. But I still flinch from being drawn into the whole political scene, which seems cruelly farcical to me. Politicians gamble without caring what the stakes are and it is the ordinary folks who are the ones being deliberately overlooked. It seems I do have political views but it has taken what has happened in England with the vote to leave the EU, and the debacle of an election here in Australia. A hung parliament is a very loud message.

But back to the poems. On Christmas Day I was distressed about a lot of things attached to that time of year, and ever vulnerable about Mark. As is often my way, I wrote a poem in anger about what happened to us in England and Ireland before we came to Australia. I wrote it for myself – or so I thought.

Stephen, ever the editor/publisher, was impressed and moved by the poem and insisted on it going in the anthology. I said I didn't want it to but he insisted. Perhaps I should have held my ground with more determination, but I didn't have what it took to fight Stephen.

I have had some comments about the poem. But for readers it is just that – a poem. For me, it was my life.

There are social issues that have touched the very core of my life and my family. There are topics that I will not ever be able to talk about academically.

I have lived in a country where, being English, I was immediately the enemy. I have been aware that two of my sons were born in 1969, and that in some countries – in particular, Ireland – so many babies born since then have grown up in a world of fear, hatred, prejudice, insane responses to insanity.

I thought we were safe coming to Australia. We were made welcome. No one cared about our background or our religious thoughts. My Irish husband was approached by the IRA within two weeks of arriving here in an attempt to enlist him in raising funds for guns for Ireland. Thankfully, and to his credit, he refused with no hesitation.

I have lived with domestic violence. I have lived with someone determined to destroy me because my thoughts were different from his. He was so hungry for power he eventually destroyed our second son.

I cannot talk academically about suicide and burying a child. My son despaired of ever getting out from under his father's control. He took a rifle and blew his brains out. He was twenty-one. He was not a child. This was the decision of a man.

Sometimes when I say my son took his own life, I find myself in some cul-de-sac with other people making the assumption that he suffered from some mental illness. He was cold sober; the autopsy showed there were no foreign substances and no mind-altering substances in his body. At 3.30 on a Friday afternoon in April, he said, 'No more'. And in an instant he was gone.

I lived through the nightmare of his funeral. I laid him in the ground as he requested. I lived the nightmare of trying to rebuild myself so I could go on living. I have done all that.

I believed I had overcome the fears and terrors that have haunted me for all my adult life. Yet *First Refuge* has undone me.

I could exercise the voice of reason. Yesterday and today are the culmination of endless, in-depth planning by a lot of people, but essentially driven by Stephen. This is all the highlight of it all.

Just as my son is not a mental illness statistic, I am not a domestic violence statistic. I know a lot about the misuse and abuse of power in an environment that should have been safe. I know a fair bit about abuse of power on a larger scale – I worked for Centrelink for twenty-five years. I see enough of the abuse of power in countries all over the world. So-called leaders of countries who let their people live in appalling conditions – for what? What are they doing with their people's wealth? It is not about how they do that, it is simply about getting off on power.

Fear breeds more fear. It is hard to break the cycle.

Friendship

Annette laughed when I said I could write a book about passion and another about love. She went quiet when I said I didn't think I could write about friendship.

I can understand her reaction. Haven't we been friends for twenty-five years? I write that and, as I place the question mark at the end of the sentence, I wonder, have we? What is a friend? What is friendship?

We hear of parents trying to be friends with their children, especially in their teenage years, but is it a friend they need? Don't they really need an authority figure to either listen to or rebel against?

As always, I come out with so many questions. And of course there is the opposite: how good a friend have I been to anyone?

I've heard it said that a friend is always there when you need them. Perhaps I need to define what I mean by friendship as I have experienced it.

In my old life, my husband was not my friend. He did not make me feel good about myself; quite the opposite, in fact. When I left him, one of my lovers was enormously helpful in practical terms and he was my friend, but it also meant I no longer wanted him as a lover.

There have been times over the years when I just needed kindness or some practical help. My lovers were not there to give me that. I was the haven for them, a place to come to be a different person from the one they had to be everywhere else. I really loved that, but there was always the secrecy – I wasn't supposed to exist in their lives.

And that is the rub, isn't it? Can lovers be friends? My experience says no. Once I have stopped being 'lover', I don't want to share any of my life with that person. Whatever intimacy we shared, once gone, then I wanted nothing more to do with them – I certainly didn't want to share my future with them. I would not have them living vicariously through me.

My relationship with Stephen is something very special and doesn't fall into any category. I understand intimacy in a very different way now. I understand commitment and constancy in a way not known before. Where in the past I have used the word 'partner', it was to ensure I had distance. I had experienced 'wife' as a possession/possessive entity with no reality other than being an extension of the other.

Yet it was me who proposed to Stephen and I knew no doubts about the decision to ask him. I have not had a moment's doubt since he said yes. And yes, I love it when he refers to me as his wife, and I love referring to him as my husband. It brings such a wonderful feeling of comfort and protection and makes a statement of guardianship. Stephen and I don't own each other but we know we look after the gift of love we have given each other in countless ways throughout our lives. If someone asked me, 'Is Stephen your friend?' the instant answer would be yes, but he is far more than that, so is the answer in fact no?

Annette I call my friend. We share something that has been built up over long years. She has dragged me screaming through the worst times in my life. She has come with me to the best times. She has infuriated me. I have ended our relationship twice yet there is something else going on here.

In 2008, Stephen agreed to publish *The Silver Cord* and I used one of her photos for the cover image. Because she had been with me when most of the poems were written, and she helped me sort out the ones to put into the manuscript, it was only right that I share my success with her. She was still in Canberra and I didn't have her phone number. I explained to my manager my predicament and he agreed to obtain her phone number for me. He wasn't breaching any confidentiality rules. I rang her and simply said, 'We've done it. We're published.'

There are so many times when I have drawn comfort from the fact that Annette knows me so well. It means there is so much I don't have to explain. Or when I am finding the past sending its long tentacles into this new life, I can talk to her to keep things in perspective and in their rightful place. I am not hiding my past from Stephen, but he said something the other day that made me realise it is all right not to talk openly about old things. I had been muttering about the circumstances of when I bought my car Pegasus. He just said, 'Has talking about the past enhanced our today?' The answer was clearly no. So don't do it. And it is as simple as that.

This takes me to another aspect of my friendship with Annette. She has always encouraged/allowed me to be weak. And there have been times when to fall in heap has been the right thing to do. But it is a place I don't want to stay. I am strong and it takes courage to live life to the fullest and I will do that. I am also aware that in many ways, at many times, she has been a substitute mother. No point in going over old ground, but the fact remains, my mother will listen to me, but she will not offer an opinion or give advice. I have to respect that and Annette has filled that need in me.

So friendship has to be a two-way street for me. It doesn't work if only one party is sharing confidences. Which takes me into the realm of friendship in this life with Stephen.

I cut all ties with people I knew before. When *The Silver Cord* was published, the people I worked with were astonished that I even wrote poetry, never mind been accepted for publication. Quite a few bought my book. I invited several to the launch and was hurt that so few came. When *It's All Good* was published, I sold very few at work, and no one came to the launch. So when I retired, I didn't want any of them coming with me.

I am uncomfortable about a woman who I used to work with. She had been so supportive at different times, and I didn't know how to embrace her in my new life. I felt disloyal to Stephen by going to see her. And she didn't seem to be able to step into my life. I was no longer a single person. Somehow being a member of a couple – properly – was an impediment to being with her. She does walk across my mind now and then, but there is an impossibility about a future for us. I have behaved badly, but I don't know how else I could have done it and I certainly have no way of bridging the gap now. I have to put my trust in the belief that if our time was not done in this life time then the gods will ensure that we meet again. Otherwise it will have to be in another lifetime.

Do I have friends in this new life? I have always been able to connect easily with men, and with male writers this is no different. It has not been so easy with women but I connect with women writers and I am certain it is the common link of writing that enables this to happen.

I started writing this thinking there was something wrong with me because I couldn't answer the question about friends. There isn't anything wrong with me. I enjoy, these days, the company of women writers, the shared hugs, the mutual encouragement, the occasional confidence but, because I have no hungers, that is enough.

My passion was burned out in one sense, but from the ashes it has grown again and found a home in what I do as a writer, with Stephen, and as part of Ginninderra Press.

Desert emptiness

I hear people talk of the emptiness of the desert and my mind immediately goes to the vast tracts of sand that all continents have. I have wanted to go to the red desert in the heart of this land. I wanted to experience only sun and wind on my skin, the featureless landscape no distraction. What did I hope for next? The same spiritual awareness or clarity such as others have known? There have certainly been many writers who have come from such an experience: not writers of novels, rather the philosophers and thinkers.

I saw the red desert from a railway carriage. It was as red as I had seen in pictures. There was the clear blue sky overhead; the land was free of any vegetation. But my spirit didn't cheer with recognition of a coming home. I was left with no questions but a sense of what next? Had I missed something? Perhaps it was simply that I was inside the railway carriage, not outside walking in the clear air.

My second attempt at experiencing the desert was again from a railway carriage. This time there wasn't the same barren land. This desert was mile after mile of saltbush. No trees, just now and then a bush that grew a little bit taller than its neighbours. The train travelled at about eighty kilometres an hour and for twelve hours we saw no trees. So that was about a thousand kilometres without a tree.

On that same trip, I had hoped to see Western Australia's famous wild flowers. The season was over before we arrived but I saw enough to witness their tenacity to grow. Nothing new there – wild flowers will grow anywhere.

What is a desert? A place where only certain things can grow. Deserts are not lifeless. Barren and desert are not synonymous. But conditions can stifle growth. What is my desert? Or should that be, where is my desert? I know this feeling of restlessness from old. A longing to stretch myself to the very edges of awareness or curl up in a ball in a dark safe place. I have plenty to occupy my mind but the satisfaction is not there. What am I creating? I am struggling to write even this musing.

It was time to stop there to make breakfast and while talking to Stephen I realised I miss the stimulation of other people at the moment. That sounds strange for me who constantly hungers for solitude. When I was at Centrelink, I was very much a loner – as in, I didn't have coffee or lunch with the girls – but I was often sought out while in the kitchenette making a cup of tea or even in the Ladies. I would be in wonderful little chats, someone talking about things that were going on in their life and they just needed to talk to get a clearer view. I loved it that my opinions were asked for, and listened to, and, after a passage of time, I was frequently told that something I had suggested worked. I was, in effect, the wise woman of the village I had always wanted to be. My village was for the most part the office where I worked.

Once I left Centrelink, I found a more active place within the world of GP and the writers therein became my village. We used to go to a lot more launches than we do these days. I loved meeting up with the authors and sharing the super experience of signing books someone had bought. There was a kindred spirit aspect to this I loved. We used to have more writers coming to our home. We have become so busy with the nuts and bolts of the business that writers don't come down or, even if they do, they come to collect books, they don't stay for a cuppa. I miss those shared times.

I love the recent exchange of emails with my brother Geoff, as his chapbook has been completed, and I always look forward to my brother Steve's letters, but their lives are so different to mine.

Sometimes I miss the people I once shared my life with – both men and women.

I moved on at the end of 2008 and none of the people I worked with wanted to come with me. They were initially surprised that my poetry was being published but beyond that nothing. But I could not have expected anything else, because my wise woman belonged in the office not in the rest of my life.

So I am a wise woman without the obvious village. My communication is mostly done via email these days. I get to know a little about the authors of the chapbooks, which I have enjoyed, but I also notice that they too often step across some invisible line and start treating me like the grocer. I withdraw at this point and become more formal.

So what's my problem? I don't think I have one. It was just a need to recognise that I miss some things out of my life, but when the time is right, other things or other people will take their place.

Solitude and silence

Growing up in a tiny English village in an old farmhouse with no electricity, silence was something I accepted as normal. My two older brothers and I seemed to spend all our daylight hours outside, no matter what the weather. We were country children and I've no doubt it was times of boredom that led to squabbles, but mostly my memories are congenial ones. On winter evenings with no television, we played card games and board games, listening to the wind howling around the chimney stacks. The house creaked and settled each night but always I remember a peaceful atmosphere.

When I had a home of my own with a husband and four lively boys, silence was a rarity. Television had limited appeal for me and I would much rather get lost in a book. As the older children grew into their teens, the various volumes of life increased and I learned I needed to seek solitude in order to have the silence.

I was given a motor scooter. I loved it – only 80cc but fully automatic, and I could fill up the tank for a couple of dollars. This was my first real step to getting away from the house while my children were at school or kindy before I joined the workforce. I covered miles and miles roaming through the hills. I could do some volunteer work. (I didn't have a licence to drive a car then and public transport was prohibitive with time.) And of course I had easy transport for when I went to do adult matric at the local TAFE college.

Many were the times I was bitterly cold and wet, but I had time to myself. I'm not sure now what my thoughts were. I remember crying a lot where no one could witness.

I joined the workforce and gradually my self-confidence grew. I always went to a nearby park to eat my lunch among the trees beside a small creek. Solitude was all I wanted. I read or daydreamed. I certainly didn't want company and my work colleagues respected that.

A friend gave me a Samoyed – Arctic Snowmist Manouk, or Kimba for general use – for my thirty-fifth birthday. It was a dog destined to be put down if not found a home and he thought I would overcome my terror of dogs if we had one. It didn't help with my fear of dogs at all, but I did have the excuse every evening to go for a walk – mostly alone. My sons respected my need for solitude and silence.

Solitude and isolation are not the same thing. Grief over my son taking his own life isolated me utterly. For the first year, shock protected me and I lived inside a bubble. I could see all that was going on around me, I went to work every day, but I wasn't part of it. Every time I tried to venture out, the words 'Mark's dead' sent me back.

Time spent alone in the car driving myself to and from work gave me solitude. Whether I cried or thought about my life, in that shell I had to share my thoughts and feelings with no one. Each morning I had to drive down a long steep hill that curved so at one point I was faced with a high, rocky hillside. I contemplated running headlong into the wall of rock every day. Once, I told a work colleague about it and from then on he made sure he was at work a few minutes before me and insisted I report in to him that I had arrived safely. It was comforting that someone cared whether I lived or died.

A few days before my fiftieth birthday, I began living alone. I took two weeks off work and I washed every item of clothing, all the bed linen and household linen. I washed curtains and scrubbed floors. I was doing everything I could to eradicate David S from the tree house. It was bliss sleeping alone. Waking up in the morning alone, getting ready for work, taking the bus to work. I found work challenging, not so much the work but having to interact with other staff members and by the time I finished at the end of the day I was exhausted from the people contact. Thirty minutes on the bus separated my worlds.

Once off the bus, I walked along the river path among the trees. I sighed with relief as I stepped through my front door. Silence. I could choose to get changed and go out for a bike ride before making a meal that suited only me. I could choose whether I listened to a talking book while I became engrossed in some artwork, or I curled up in a chair and watched a DVD. I could choose to go to bed early, particularly in the winter, and read a book snuggled up and warm.

It was at work that I became aware I was the wise woman. I refused to hide the facts that I had been a badly battered person who had been driven from her home by a strong sense of survival and that my son had taken his own life. I listened when colleagues talked to me and offered an opinion based on my personal experience. I always qualified my words with 'When this happened to me, I did or said this', or 'My mother taught me…'

The gift of words has been a blessing. I disappear into my own world and I know I become quite insular while I am writing. I have learned that I can read or write anywhere, no matter what is going on around me. Even now, in a wonderful relationship with Stephen where silence is a key part of our lives, I still wake early and do as I am doing now, sitting in the cosy corner reading or writing. I love to sit in the garden to write. It depends on my mood. Sometimes I choose to sit in the walled garden, where I have a sense of seclusion, or other times I sit on the riverside, where I can watch the life on the tidal reach and also be aware of people walking past.

The gods were kind when they sent Stephen into my life. He likes to listen to Classic FM while he is working, but the radio is on so quietly I can barely hear it when I tap on the office doorway when I need to consult him about something. We finish work at about four in the afternoon and we sit in the cosy corner after our bike ride and read in companionable silence.

But real silence is the absence of sound. Even now, I have the quiet hum of the water cooler or the fridge close by in the kitchen and outside I can hear the rain falling. Trains trundle over the bridge and we have become so used to them I rarely notice them consciously; it is the same with distant traffic or very occasionally a plane. Fortunately, there is not much of any of them.

If I go out on my bike to the beach, there is the sound of the wind and the constant shushing of the water. In the garden, there is always the sound of birds calling or the wind in the trees. I love to walk through wooded areas.

Silence for me is the absence of voices. I weary of voices a lot. They are so often harsh and intrusive, people talking about anything rather than have to listen to their thoughts. I am not afraid of the thoughts in my head. I am not afraid to put my thoughts down on paper for others to read.

Spirituality

There is another perception of home for me. It is spiritual.

I have no interest in organised religion. I have no interest in discussing heaven and hell. These are all man-made constructs to keep people in line.

I have had a lifelong love and appreciation of nature. For years I felt like a dandelion, taproot going deep into the earth and very, very hard to eradicate – ask any gardener – while my face was held up to the sun. I was very trusting like a flower. There is not much a flower can do to protect itself from everything around it.

Then as I grew older and my life grew bigger, I felt more like a tree. I liked the image of all kinds of life finding safety and refuge with me. Still trusting and vulnerable but a bit tougher than a flower.

Somewhere along the way, I could see my life as a road and I was heading for the sun. I might detour along many winding side-tracks, have to cross waterways on precariously balanced rocks at times, but always I was heading for the sun. This was influenced by thinking about the sun-worshippers of old. What could be more simple than their lives? Everything happened in relation to the sun, moon and changing seasons. I still watch the sunrise and the sunset as often as possible. I have stood on the beach watching the sun sink into the ocean and known that moment of pure terror linked to that fleeting flash of brilliant blue light, wondering if the sun will return, or will life simply end in the darkness of night? When life has been relentless with terror, anger and grief, I have watched the sun rising, wishing it wasn't, yet at the same time being in awe of the gift of another day.

What those ancient sun worshippers did not know perhaps and I do is that the sun is the heart of this universe. Without it, there would be nothing. Their instincts to worship the sun in the hope or belief that this would ensure another day, another season, is very easy to for me to understand.

The sun influences everything I do. I live in a country where the sun shines pretty much every day. I find that a couple of days with overcast skies makes my spirits plummet. I am the first to admit I love the wind and rain, but not the seemingly endless rainy grey days I remember in England.

With the onset of global warming, I fear the sun these days. As I write this, we have had seven consecutive months of slightly but consistently higher temperatures. The wind blows from a different direction, not so much from the south-west any more, which brings the cold from the Antarctic. What will happen to our rainfall? What will happen in this state with less water? The questions are far too many, far too serious and unanswerable.

The sun is still my spirit's home. There are times when I weary of life – even this good one. I have said I have lived a rich full life but it is small wonder I get weary at times. And I find myself sighing that I want to go home. But where is home? Not the old farmhouse; that has been changed almost beyond recognition and I have no claim to it in any way – except in my heart and through beautiful childhood memories.

Home for my spirit is as indescribable as the sun. I have no idea what happens when we die. When my dad and my son died, I put them in a wood walking together in harmony because that is what I needed for both of them and me. It is an image that brings comfort to the grief. I will place Mother there when the time comes, and my brothers. Do I see myself walking with them? Perhaps by then instead of walking through the trees with filtered light, I will see the brightness ahead and know that we are all moving towards home, the sun.

I have stated that I have no interest in organised religion. The holy books are filled with sensible guides for living, wonderful stories of mythology, but as a writer I cannot believe that any of them are the words of a god. Someone tried to explain the Koran to me and he believed without doubt that it was the word of God gifted to Mohammed, and all the prayers and text are still in the original language. My response was that, even if I accepted that that happened, it was still Mohammed who took the words from his head or heart and committed them to paper. How can anyone know how faithfully he did that and how much was his own interpretation of what he heard? Added to this mistrust, I have since read that Mohammed could not read or write and the scribes wrote down what he told them. How unreliable is all that! These are unanswerable questions and it does come down to a matter of faith – faith being very different to belief. Faith is something that cannot be defined, it is a gift; if you don't have it, no one can explain it, and if you do, then no explanation is required.

At the time after my son died when I was consciously rebuilding myself by questioning all my standards and values, I knew I needed somewhere to direct my thanks. I have said many times it was the natural world that was the only constant in my life, so it became inevitable, I suppose, that I too became a sun worshipper. More than that, though, I became very aware of the nightly changing strength of the moon. She seemed to represent life, constantly changing yet in some way ensuring that things stayed the same.

So it was to the moon that I sent my prayers. Every day I still give thanks for my beautiful loves, my babies, my family and my friends. I give thanks for an amazing life, a brave heart and the words. But I am still only a person and I have times of fragility and so I ask for help, to keep myself centred, that my faith I will have what is right for me when it is right is strengthened, and lastly I pray for the courage to grasp each opportunity as it arises to live life to the fullest.

There are times when life seems to send inexplicable challenges to those I love. I am able to step back to assess what I can actually do to help and, beyond some practical things, I resort to prayer. I don't ask that the challenge pass them by, rather I pray they will have the courage they need to deal with the challenge.

Body art and spirituality may seem an odd partnership but for myself I know they are linked.

I don't know the origins of tattoos. Since time beyond measure, people have decorated their bodies. For some, it was 'paint' made from the multicoloured rocks and soils where they lived. For some, it was ritual cuts that left a particular type of scar that was a recognised part of the rites of passage for the young to become adults.

Tattoos are created by the skin being broken and dye being added to the cut so with the healing the scar remains coloured. No matter how sophisticated the techniques have become, essentially nothing has changed.

Tattoos make a statement of who someone is. I remember my mother telling me a story about her father. He was in the navy possibly during World War I. His ship went to India and he had a couple of tattoos done – one being a signet ring on his little finger – something my mother says she has always wanted too. She says sailors were encouraged to have tattoos when they went to the tropics as their bodies while healing built up an added immunity to the diseases rampant in that climate. I don't know if that is a fact, but it does have credibility.

As I've said, getting a tattoo for young men seems to have been a mark of accepting personal hardship perhaps to prove courage. But what is it for women? I can only answer that from my own experience. Why and when?

After my son died, twenty-five years go at the time of writing, I felt my arms had been wrenched from their sockets. It was a physical pain, an ache that nothing could assuage. About ten years after he died, I found myself living alone. I decided to make real the longing to have a candle flame tattooed at the top of my right arm. I found there were so many times I hugged myself and to have this flame of light to touch, a physical thing, helped centre the pain till I found comfort and so release it. It is hard to describe it in a way that others might understand – it is another of those faith things.

Although I lived alone, I did have several lovers. One of them felt like he was the other half of my soul. He made me a whole person. Ours was a complicated relationship and I find I don't want to give details. It was absolutely right for us and continued on and off for twenty years before I ended it. Some lovers carve their names or initials in a tree or on a rock. I chose to have his name tattooed on my leg. I had both of these tattoos done at the same appointment. The tattoo artist was hesitant because in those times women wearing tattoos was not as accepted as it is now. He pointed out that I would not be allowed in some places with the candle flame on display. And what happened if the relationship ended and I had this name on my leg? I was determined to have my own way and he did as I asked. I have to say my lover hadn't believed I would go through with it and was torn between admiration and horror.

Time passed and I decided to have two more tattoos done. The red and yellow flame was the obvious fire. The name represented water/emotion. I chose to have a moth placed close to the flame. This was air/flight but also how I am drawn to the fire of love. I designed a cluster of oak leaves and acorns for the symbol for earth. They were gold and bronze, the colours of autumn. I thought they were preferable to having a mountain. So there I had my earth, fire, air and water. I was and continue to be a pagan at heart and this was my statement. Others could love me or leave me alone.

With the further passage of time, I was gifted a new life. I could not hide the name on my leg but I was troubled by it. I told Stephen that I had been totally committed to the name but religious and racial intolerance were alive and well and I had ended the association. I also said I would answer any questions he had honestly but I would not volunteer any information. Stephen has always respected that. He did tease me for a while but learned I wouldn't respond and he hasn't done it since. After much soul-searching, I chose the shape of a baby seal to cover the name. It was very painful to have done both physically and emotionally. When the tattoo artist had finished, I could see he hadn't done it properly and there is something shark-like about the mouth. I felt there was some kind of retribution in that and will not have it amended.

There lingered an unrest. For years, I wanted a tattoo of the moon but couldn't work out where to place it. I had read about a tribe of women who had a crescent moon tattooed on their faces but I knew this wasn't right for me. Only a few weeks ago, I decided to have my candle flame touched up and, from who knows where, I knew I wanted a crescent moon embracing my candle flame. Even though my life is filled with love and harmony, there are still times when I hug myself. With this new tattoo, I could touch the moon for courage and comfort as a physical action not just a prayer.

It was a different tattoo artist and while I looked through the images I instantly fell in love with the crescent moon intermingled with stars. It is a constant source of comfort for me. Stephen was rather dazed at first, but there was no point in being unpleasant about it, I had done it without talking to him about it. This was my body and I would do what I wanted. As it happens, no one will know any of my tattoos are on my body unless I deliberately show them.

In a general way, I have mixed views about body art. Like countless phases over the years, young people have worn certain hairstyles or clothes, listened to certain music. It is our modern-day rite of passage making some kind of statement about who we are. Wearing your hair pink and having half-a-dozen piercings are things that can be easily undone. Tattoos are not. Small ones done for a dare, I can understand. Names of loved ones, I can understand. One of my sons has a treble clef on his arm. Where I am uncomfortable is the latest trend for arms or legs completely covered in tattoos. Some even go so far as to have their entire bodies covered. I stand at the supermarket check-out looking at these sometimes and it is so hard to see what theme or message there is. It seems like so much colour used to fill a space. I might be wrong; perhaps the owners have laboured long over choosing the images they want.

At the risk of sounding completely hypocritical, I really dislike these mass tattoos on girls and women. If they were part of a traditional culture, I think I would be more at ease, but these seem to be used as a way to hide who the owner is rather than enhance or make a clear statement about who they are.

But perhaps too this is how traditions are born. A few people do something to be different and before long there is a following of people who want to emulate that rather than finding their own way. There is one niggling doubt in my mind, that our young people have little concept of time, or a future. In a 'live now because there won't be tomorrow' global pattern, why would they give thought to looking after ourselves and our planet to make sure there is a tomorrow?

I have always been wary of my ability to be inside another person's space. What a stupid word that is but for the moment I don't know how to describe what I mean. I have long known and accepted that I can go to the middle of someone instantly on meeting and I know them. Not what their likes and dislikes are or fine details, but somewhere on a different level of awareness, I am at one with them. This has crossed all surface barriers of colour, race, gender and age. This connection is on a plane that I suspect is beyond words.

It has been rare that the ones I have connected with have refused to acknowledge the connection, but it has not always lead to conversations or deep and meaningful exchanges. But we know it is absolutely right.

Such a connection was made this year with an Aboriginal man, at a book launch. There were no words. We didn't even make eye contact except very briefly when we were introduced and again when he left. While he was composing himself to make a speech to launch the book, I glanced his way. He sat in a world of his own while being surrounded by chattering voices. I slipped into the plane of awareness he was in. He knew I was there and I retreated immediately, calling to the Earth Mother.

It wasn't the connection that troubled me but why I called to the Earth Mother. She has been how I have identified myself for most of my adult life and she has been the heart of my sensuality. When it was time to change my way of living, I stopped worshipping the Earth Mother and prayed only to the moon.

When Stephen took me to the Northern Territory, I found my connection with the earth again and it was the spirits who lived there who embraced me. We were on a river that ran through a deep gorge. The Aboriginal guide had done something that has not happened to me before – he looked properly into my eyes. Whatever he saw in mine, he accepted me. He coloured a mark on the back of my hand from ochre and although it washed off very soon afterwards, I felt it was as lasting as any of my other tattoos. In the silence that followed, I knew peace and acceptance. From then, I felt this country was my extended garden and I was not afraid to see more of it.

We travelled across the Hay Plain and during the night I met an elderly Aboriginal woman; she was my sister. We went to Tasmania and in the north-western areas I met my family, the elder at Dismal Swamp, the young warriors who were my brothers and the laughing little girl who took my hand as we walked beside a rushing river. How real they all were.

Our trip to Western Australia cast me adrift again. The connection I had felt with the earth and the spirits disappeared. It had something to do with what had happened to the earth and the people with the coming of white people. I have been in a state of shock since I witnessed the destruction of life. First from the plane I looked down at the great circles of white sand. I didn't know they were salt pans. We went for a day trip to Wave Rock and drove through mile after mile of grain, but there was no sign of wild life or even the farmers tending the crops. Apparently the early settlers cleared all the trees to grow the grain. In doing that, they upset the natural balance of the underground water table and now the salt is rising. There were areas of reforestation but it may well be too late.

From the top of Wave Rock, I could see the surrounding land and, for as far as I could see, it was dried up and barren. We went to a cave where the local Aboriginal people had lived and I could not even sense their presence even though there were hands painted on the cave walls.

I went to Western Australia hoping to experience the desert and I did, but not what I thought. I experienced the desert created by white men. Even though we returned to Adelaide on the Indian Pacific and I saw the purity of the real desert from the train, I couldn't connect as I had hoped.

As I have been recalling these events and feelings, I think the meeting with the man at the book launch was meant to be my reconnection with the Earth Mother and a renewal or reaffirmation that I have been accepted here. The Aboriginal people who are alive today may feel anger and hatred towards me because of my colour and what has happened in the past, but I have not knowingly hurt any of their people or tried to intrude on their spirituality or their connection with the land.

Tolerance

No unscrambling eggs.

I am troubled by the history of this country, how the whites treated the indigenous people, and I was shocked when I talked to Stephen about it. I acknowledged that some of my thoughts were callous and cynical, then I paused for a moment and Stephen teased, 'Racist.' Am I?

I am vocally scathing of the English and their arrogance wherever they have gone in the world building the Empire. It seems I have the same arrogance for all that I have lived here for forty-five years and living with Stephen and his very socialist philosophy for the past seven years.

Growing up in England I didn't think of myself as English until I married an Irishman. I quickly learned, in my short time living in Ireland, of the hatred the Irish have for the English and, with my sparse knowledge of history, it seems justified. But the Irish as a nation do seem to take pride in their ability to hold a grudge. From my reading of history, they are also an essentially war-loving people. In ancient times, the country was divided into kingdoms and there didn't appear to be much tolerance shown. Brian Baru united the tribes against outside invaders – Normans or Romans, I can't remember – and when that threat was averted, he said something like 'I'm off back home to make love to my wife', and the tribes went back to fighting each other.

I was only nineteen when we went to Dublin and with my naive sensitivities I felt I was being blamed for the awful things the English had done to the Irish for the past eight hundred years. It is something that has stayed with me. But the intolerance I experienced at the hands of the Irish wasn't just because I was English. I was not a Catholic and in Dublin in 1969 that was almost as bad as being English. I think that was where my dislike of organised religion began.

I have sons born in England and Ireland. In London, my children's father had difficulty finding a priest who would baptise our eldest because I wasn't a Catholic and we hadn't been married in the church.

About three months later, we moved to Dublin. I knew I was pregnant again and the doctor I saw referred me to one of the hospitals. I was told that their policy was that if there were problems with either the pregnancy or the delivery, then they would save the life of the baby not the mother. I could see the possibility of my children's father being left a widow with two motherless babies. It didn't make sense to me and I went to another hospital.

When my second son was ten days old, the lady across the road came and took him away to be baptised. I trailed along and the priest refused me entry into the church – not even for the blessing of the mothers which is part of the ceremony. I skulked outside the church with our first-born and silently questioned the Christian ethic as I had been shown it.

I don't know how many of the difficulties in my marriage resulted from the difference in our backgrounds. I was often heard to say we couldn't have been more different if one of us had been black.

In my early years in Australia, I was friends with a woman from Dublin. She was married to an Englishman and they had nine children and were very devout Catholics. They were able to live a much more tolerant life together. But Sally also educated me a bit about the way things were in much of the Ireland of her era and before. It was interesting that she disagreed with that strongly.

Mothers treated their sons like kings in the making. They came first in everything. They had the lion's share of food regardless of how little there was and how many in the family needed to be fed. Boys were educated rather than girls. Girls were taught to put males first in everything. When a man went out to work, he expected to do whatever he wanted with his wages. If he was a gambling or drinking man, it was a race at the works gate on a Friday night whether the wife managed to get the money off him or whether he escaped by some back way and went down to the pub.

My children's father's family told me stories about their own father as if it were all a joking matter. Their mother died of a heart attack at the age of fifty-two. No one seemed to want to talk about the connection with the strain of trying to look after her family and her early death. It seemed easier to be maudlin over the fact she had died.

But no matter how badly their menfolk behaved, the wife was expected to be forgiving: 'Ah, the poor thing, he can't help himself' being the common outlook. I was fortunate that my Irishman was more considerate in many ways and he always ensured there was enough money to keep a roof over our heads, food on the table and clothes on our backs. But then I haven't ever considered him a typical Irishman.

The Irish do have a certain capacity to laugh at themselves, have a wonderful store of legends and mythologies and a charming way with music and lyrics, but I trip over the whole concept that the men must be treated like naughty children to be accommodated because they can't help themselves. There is too much self-indulgence and subsequent family suffering in that for my taste.

It is interesting that while working for the Public Service I encountered many men and women from different places in the world. The Islamic people and many people from the southern and eastern European countries have similar beliefs regarding how women treat their menfolk and I was shocked again to be on the receiving end of religious and racial intolerance.

I was largely ignorant of Australian history when I came here to live. While I admit to enjoying my history when couched in a novel, I found that in the few historical novels I did read set in the early colonial years, the stories were boring and essentially 'all the same'. Somehow I had not found one that touched on the lot of the Aboriginal people at all.

I had no contact with Aboriginal people until in my years working for a government agency I became aware that at some primal level I was frightened of them. I was meeting them in the worst of conditions from their perspective. Lost between worlds. The traditions of the past gone and no place in the society and its rules that were thrust upon them. Like the Irish, they have every reason to be angry. My fear was of doing something wrong – albeit inadvertently – and triggering some kind of revenge on a plane that was not physical. Although I knew nothing of Aboriginal legends or mythology, I had heard about 'pointing the bone' and that was what I feared.

My Australian-born son had a troubled relationship with a young woman who was part-Aboriginal. I don't know the details; I think the bloodline was traced back to her grandmother. When the eldest of their two sons was born, I realised suddenly I had a link to this country that I hadn't felt before. Although these two little boys were as blonde and green/blue-eyed as their mother, I was quietly proud that they could claim Aboriginal blood. I felt less of an intruder to this land.

I still don't understand why I felt this. From the moment I stepped off the plane in November 1970 and looked at the sleeping Adelaide Hills, I felt I was home. Yet it took the birth of my grandsons to feel something more definable than an instinct.

How fortunate I was that Stephen introduced me to a new and more enlightened view of Australian literature through *Capricornia* and *Poor Fellow My Country*, both written by Xavier Herbert. I became more aware of the complexities of blacks, whites, and Asians and the impossible dilemma of the 'mixed-bloods'.

I have since gone on to read a number of books about the ignorance and outrageous cruelty between the settlers and the Indigenous people: the unsolvable issues of differing values, the helplessness becoming anger and bigotry, fear and hatred being the strongest things to survive.

I started out wondering if I was a racist. I'm not. My friend suggests I am angerist – I am anti anger and conflict.

As sure as I know anything in this life, violence has not ever resolved differences or relieved pain. It is only one person inflicting power over another with no respect – and too often escalating to become outright war on human dignity.

Yes, I am hurt by intolerance wherever I encounter it. There is no such thing as simply black or white. It is important to hold views and stand by them. There are times when it is important to stand up and be counted.

There is no definitive solution to the issue of mixed blood. We are all people. Regardless of traditions and beliefs, the soul of a woman is forever changed once she has known that new life is within her body. The soul of a man is forever changed when he learns he has fathered a child. Men and women are forever changed when their child dies. These things can be called animal instinct but they are also what makes us human.

We must respect ourselves first in order to be able to respect others. Only then will we be shown respect.

Yes, I get impatient with the frailties of the human condition – especially my own – but I hope not to the point of being disrespectful and intolerant.

Immediate joy

I wanted to write about love and friendship but found when it came to it I wasn't sure what I knew about either.

I could have written about passion and instincts. As my life has been driven by them one way or another, that would have been easy to do. As for friendship, I was on very shaky ground. So I abandoned that chapter and remembered immediate joy.

Having been influenced by many books over the years, I am happy to acknowledge *A Boy Named Bracken* by Elizabeth Webster to be the most inspirational of all. It opened my eyes to the simple concept of immediate joy. I will even confess that, unable to find it in bookshops and being the time before the ease of internet shopping, I kept the copy I had found in my local library and cheerfully paid the bill I was sent for the 'lost' book. I am sorry that by doing that I have deprived other readers of the book's magic and I don't know how to amend that, except perhaps to live the immediate joy and hope others see that and try and do it too.

The book was set in the early sixties in Gloucestershire – not so far from where I grew up – therefore I had an instant and comforting connection with the countryside as provided by the author's vivid descriptions. I knew how beech woods grow. I have walked in meadows where grasses dance with dewdrop diamonds gleaming in the sun of a 'pearly morning'. I knew about narrow lanes and high hedges. I knew about the life of farmers and the ever-present dangers to their livelihood. I knew about their complicated relationships with gypsies and their mixed views on badgers. I knew about the silence that is no silence in the country.

The story was about Jake, a man who had only weeks to live, and against that dark backdrop I found another link. His lesson in immediate joy became mine. It was late spring when Jake's doctor told him the cancer had returned and he would not see the end of summer. His wish to just disappear was fulfilled when he rented a tiny cottage from Carol, a work colleague's sister, and he went to the depths of the countryside to lick his wounds and quietly die. There were many times after my difficult marriage ended and one of my sons took his own life that I wanted to do just that.

Jake was in his fifties and as a journalist had travelled to many places in the world and seen first-hand the devastation of wars and the plight of desperate people left to rebuild their lives from the ashes. In my time working for Centrelink, I met people from all walks of life and learned that poverty of spirit was evident on both sides of the counter.

Jake's dedication to his career had cost him his marriage. Rather than cause angst to his son and daughter, he had walked away from conflict with their mother and her materialistic attitude and provided whatever monies were needed to ensure they had a good home and education.

As soon as Jake arrived at the cottage, he encountered Bracken, an eleven- or twelve-year-old gypsy who invited him to go for a walk at dawn the next day. And so began Jake's education about life and joy.

Bracken introduced Jake to Blackie the blackbird living in the pear tree in the garden. When Blackie was frantic one quiet afternoon because a magpie was after his eggs, Jake became aware of the daily struggle for survival that even the smallest of creatures were up against.

Bracken cut the grass in the cottage garden, freed the flowers from weeds and planted some quick-growing vegetables. They discovered there was a hedgehog living in the garden and started leaving milk out for it.

Jake and Bracken often walked down to the nearby lake to watch the swans in the very early morning light and up into the woods to watch the badgers in the moonlight.

They set up a temporary aviary in the garden to house an injured kestrel and later when the kestrel was well enough to be freed into the wild this was converted to a home for a young orphaned badger who needed time to grow a little more before it was able to fend for itself in the wild.

Jake was embraced by the small neighbouring community and

Bracken's gypsy family. This was a time in England when neither badgers or gypsies were welcomed. Each day was taken as it came and he did as much as his weakening condition allowed him to do. The weight of despair was lightened and Jake was being healed even as he was dying.

I didn't have an aviary, a badger cub or English countryside, but I did live in a small house on a hillside that felt as if I was living in the tree tops. I fed the birds breadcrumbs and seeds and watched in wonder as they came down onto my balcony to feed even as I sat there reading or having my breakfast. I had a small vegetable garden to grow tomatoes and snow peas. I had flower beds and ivy-covered walls. I was surrounded by green.

I looked out of my window into the eyes of a koala. I saw four sacred ibis dancing like ballerinas on my lawn. I listened to the kookaburras calling to each other in what sounded like heated discussions. I've seen the river at the bottom of the garden nothing more than a succession of puddles and also like a raging wild animal as flood waters broke the banks and ducks floated on what the day before had been a patch of grass and now was an extension of the river.

I had the constant pattern of sunrise and sunset filling my home with colour. I had stillness and the sharp crack of bark breaking in the heat, and the sound of strong winds through the trees and the tension of wondering if the trees would fall on my roof. I have woken in the night to my home flooded in moonlight so bright I could sit by the window and write a poem about it.

Yes, I wept a lot but I had all those moments of immediate joy too.

Jake's friend and work colleague went to see Jake's children, who were in their early twenties and in the process of finishing their education. When they learned their father was dying, they reluctantly agreed to go to see him at the cottage. A meeting was set up and it was a revelation to Jake to find he really liked the people his children had grown to be and that each in their own way was using his own approach to life and work as a guide. Without his constant presence, he had thought they would have similar standards and values to their mother – that material things, not people, were the most important things in life.

I have been astounded and humbled to learn that as my children have grown beyond the callous, judgemental years and have become parents and mature adults themselves, they have admiration for their parents. It was a big thing to come to the other side of the world to live with no other family here for support. They are pleased that I found the strength to make a life of my own and that my dreams have come true – to share my life with someone of like mind and to be a published writer. But the most heart-warming was their pleasure at the announcement that Stephen and were going to get married. They were delighted that I was happy.

There was another aspect to immediate joy for Jake to learn. Carol called in with her twin sons aged about ten. They were all enchanted by the little badger and by Jake and Bracken. Their own struggle to survive the loss of their father/husband was given a new aspect. Carol found that she was capable of loving again even in those unusual circumstances or perhaps because of them. Jake too finds a capacity for a love he had only dreamed of ever knowing.

Perhaps the most powerful lesson for both Jake and Bracken to learn was what they were prepared to do for love of a friend.

Bracken overheard a farmer saying he was going to smoke out a nearby badger sett and kill the animals. Bracken risked his own life to get there before the farmer and frighten the badgers away. He saw the mother badger shot and he was able to gather a young one and hide it in his jacket and fled before the hunting dogs. He kept running and eventually fell down into a quarry. Jake became concerned when Bracken hadn't come for his usual visit and more so when Bracken's father came to the cottage to ask after his son. It was following an instinct that Jake set off to find his young friend. Against all odds he does find the unconscious Bracken and had to carry him back to the gypsy camp. He collapsed just as Bracken's father found them.

Of course this is how the orphaned badger came to live in Jake's garden. Bracken risked his life for the badgers because of his love of life. Jake risked his life to find his young friend whom he knew to be in danger.

The story ended with the return of the kestrel to Jake's garden and the birds urgent calls, a plea that Jake follow him. Jake followed the bird for miles till he came across the kestrel's mate caught in a trap. Jake died using the last of his strength freeing the bird.

I could misquote something from the Bible about there being no greater love than a man give up his life…

For the past twenty-five years, I have tried to make my son's death count for something. He may have taken his life in a time of despair, but his brothers and I have all become better people because of it.

I seem to have come back to love. Not romantic love. Dare I say a love that is deeper because its very roots are in nobility? We have a greater appreciation of the fragility of life. We know the finality of death. We have fought bitterness, grief and anger and come through.

Yes, I know how to experience joy but my ability to laugh is still precarious. I have found life to be very serious. To laugh seems irresponsible somehow. I have been the one to openly acknowledge many times that I have laughed more with Stephen than I have in the rest of my life. But it doesn't come easily and I don't know if it ever will.

I can smile quietly to myself and do often. I can go to the beach and play in the waves till I laugh out loud like a child. I can sometimes laugh at a joke. Perhaps it is that I find it hard to laugh at someone and a situation they might be in. Laughing with someone and laughing at someone: there is world of difference between the two.

Quiet joy. Immediate joy. These for me are far better than hilarity.

Wholeness

When Alex, my eldest son, was about thirteen or fourteen, he brought home his first girlfriend. I took an instant dislike to her. It had nothing to do with her big green eyes or the blonde hair. It was something far more basic than that. She had taken Alex's attention away from me. It wouldn't have mattered who she was, and I'm not even sure, if I had liked her more, whether my reaction would have been any different.

I recognised in that moment of introduction that he was no longer going to tell me his thoughts first. Whether it was this girl or another one, he would be talking to someone other than me. I found that incredibly painful. I could see also that I was going to be an over-possessive mother and I needed to be careful or I would alienate my sons from me and that was the last thing I wanted. I stepped back and counselled myself to get used to it. But I wonder now if perhaps I wasn't asking too much of myself.

Walking along the beach this morning, I contemplated being a mother. It isn't something that can be put on and off like an article of clothing when it suits.

From the moment a female, regardless of age, knows she is carrying a child, she is forever changed. She is no longer, and will not ever in this lifetime be, a single person. Abortion or miscarriage may end the pregnancy but it won't wind back time or unknow knowledge. The body, the mind and the spirit know there was another person who was part of them and there will always be a hunger to hold that person.

I think for me, the sweetest times have been when a child of mine has fallen asleep in my arms. It is the closest I could get to that time before they were born, and no one could deny that, for that brief period of time, the unborn child was mine. Once they were born, the link was no longer physical but it was replaced by an ache in my arms.

I didn't really know it was that until Mark died and I felt my arms had been pulled out of their sockets. I still feel that awful tug like a physical pain. When I am distressed, I wrap my arms around myself and hold my shoulders as if to ease the pain.

It took a long time to accept that when Mark died part of me died. I didn't just grieve because of the reasons he took his own life, I grieved that his life had ended. True, I instantly thought when I was told he was dead that I could stop worrying about him, he was out of it all and I was pleased for him. But as time went inexorably on, I grieved for the children of Mark that would never look at me with his green eyes. His life was not going to unfold. The part of me that was Mark had ended. It couldn't grow without him.

I could come across photographs of him I had forgotten, or not even known had been taken, but that only enriched my memories; it didn't give me something new. I have listened to his brothers talking about him and learned all sorts of different things about who he was and what he did, but again it only enriched the memories (and I am always glad to gather the extra gems). I love it when I see echoes of him in photographs of my dad and my brothers – but then I feel that when I see Mark's brothers in the same people. I love the family gene pool that reaches back to who knows where and will extend forward to who knows where.

What was more important today was the recognition of grief over my living sons. They had to grow up without me from the time Mark died. I didn't deliberately do it. I was in such a deep state of shock – shock not just over him but being battered and beaten by their father for far too many years before I had the courage and wherewithal to leave. I was filled with terror each time I saw them that it would be the last time, and, whether to protect me or his own interests, David S, my partner of the time, kept them away. By the time I could separate myself from him, so much damage had been done to us all.

They have done what I believe is right for them. They grew up and entered relationships of their own. No doubt they have each looked for someone who could create a warm and loving home with them. I did this for myself too and have at last achieved that with someone who shares the same wants and needs.

So what is the hunger that lingers and has turned into grief, a dull ache as in my shoulders and my missing arms?

I have missed out on so much of their lives. Some was naturally going to happen but what happened to my family was not. All families are torn by conflict. Sometimes it comes from outside the family unit, in the shape of disruptive influences and outright war. Sometimes it is the clash of personalities that means members are unable to be friends. It has been said you can choose your friends but not your family. I have watched this in action since the boys were in their early teens when Noel J said he admired the way Alex and Mark were finding their individual ways but he didn't want to do what either of them were doing. I admired his perception and his courage to say this out loud.

With Mark, my arms were there one minute, gone the next. With the other three, my arms, my mind and my spirit have been starving and withering away. I feel a terrible weariness that is hard to lighten despite so much being so very good in my life.

These past months, I have thought and written so much about my parents and my own childhood family. There is a strong sense of connection that has precious little to do with contact and there are times they seem a very long way away, but I don't want to go back to England to see them and have to leave them again. While watching a program on TV recently, I saw something in Devonshire that I connected with and if ever the day comes when I need to go somewhere alone, I will go there and not return to Australia. With that recognition, I no longer feel I am trapped with nowhere to go and so I can allow myself to feel the joy again that recent circumstances seems to have diminished somewhat.

Now I have recognised the weariness regarding my children, I can find ease to the pain.

When all is said and done, I may not see them very often, but nothing can undo or destroy the good years we shared when they were little and I was the centre of their universe. Nothing can destroy the fact that I am not just Brenda. There is so much more to me than that. While I am solitary when I walk along the beach or stand on the balcony in the early morning to watch the day wake up and dolphins appear looking for breakfast, I am not alone. I am a complete and whole person. If the gods are kind, there will be other people who will come into my life and add to this wholeness but I am not less because I haven't met them yet.

www.ingramcontent.com/pod-product-compliance
Lightning Source LLC
Chambersburg PA
CBHW030916080526
44589CB00010B/336